Ne~ k

ɢreeting Cards

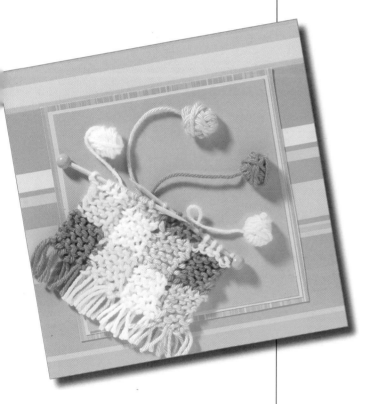

**Margriet Kors and
Gina Kors-Lambers**

FORTE PUBLISHERS

Contents

Second printing, May 2006
ISBN 90 5877 627 1

This is a publication from
Forte Publishers BV
P.O. Box 1394
3500 BJ Utrecht
The Netherlands

For more information about the creative
books available from Forte Publishers:
www.forteuitgevers.nl

Final editing: Gina Kors-Lambers,
Steenwijk, the Netherlands
Photography and digital image
editing: Fotografie Gerhard Witteveen,
Apeldoorn, the Netherlands
Cover and inner design: BADE creatieve
communicatie, Baarn, the Netherlands
Translation: Michael Ford, TextCase,
Hilversum, the Netherlands

Preface

This book follows on from the success of the book "Knit-it Greeting Cards". The name says exactly what the technique involves and this book is filled with many cheerful cards for many different occasions.

We have tried to make it even more fun to make knit-it cards. By not only using normal cotton, but also Funny Fibres, Wire & Wire and paper yarn, the cards become surprisingly different. We have also used some new patterns. We think it is a great book and hope that you have as much fun making the cards as we did.

Have fun!

Margriet and Gina

Techniques

Knitwear
This book contains several different items of knitwear which you can make using many different types of yarn. Use no. 2 knitting needles.

Stocking stitch
Plain knit one row and then purl knit one row.

Ribs
Plain knit all the rows.

Reducing stitches at the start of a row
Slip off one stitch at the start of the row (transfer it to the right-hand knitting needle without knitting the stitch), knit one stitch and then pull the slipped stitch over the stitch which has just been knitted.

Knit two stitches together at the end of the row.

Adding stitches
Cast on extra stitches at the end of each row. Knit the stitches in the next row.

Knitting holes
Knit on the right-hand side (good side) of the knitwear. Knit one stitch, move the yarn forwards and plain knit two stitches together. The yarn will fall like a collar around the needle. Knit this collar in the next row.

Making a cord

Make a loop in one or more of the threads of yarn. Place this loop (or loops) around a door handle. Twist the yarn. Thread something heavy (such as a pair of scissors) onto the twisted yarn. Take the loop off of the door handle and hold the ends together. The pair of scissors will twist the yarn into a cord. Tie a knot in the ends and cut the scissors loose.

Making a tassel

Wind the yarn onto your fingers or a piece of card. Tie the end securely around the ball. Cut through the loops.

Finishing

Once you have finished the knitwear, cut off the cast-on yarn. Cut off the knitting yarn so that it is 50 cm long.

Place the knitwear on cocktail sticks and use Aleene's Thick Designer Tacky glue to stick wooden beads on the ends. Roll the long knitting yarn into a ball or wind it around a piece of card. Use Aleene's Thick Designer Tacky glue to stick the knitwear on the card. Use Make Me jewellery glue to stick Wire & Wire and a bag clip together and to stick them on the card.

Materials

- Catania knitting yarn
- Various Funny Fibres
- Wire & Wire
- Twistart paper yarn
- Inox knitting needles (no. 2)
- Make Me wooden beads (Ø 6 mm)
- Card: cArt-us and Cardstock

- Making Memories embellishment paper
- Aleene's Thick Designer Tacky glue
- Make Me photo glue
- Make Me jewellery glue
- Make Me easy punch: various shapes

- Frances M. letter stickers: Fun
- Make Me pompoms: 5 mm
- Cutting mat
- Make Me design knife
- Quilt ruler
- Pencil
- Eraser

Step-by-step

1. Materials for making Knit-it cards.

2. Thread Rocailles onto Wire & Wire.

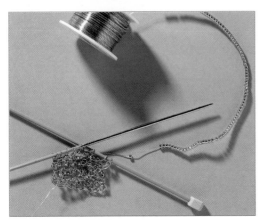

3. Knitting using Wire & Wire and Rocailles.

4. Transfer the stitches onto cocktail sticks with wooden beads.

Fun

Sweater

What you need

- Card: cArt-us orange (0545); Cardstock silvery white metallic gloss (9201) and saffron (2090); Making Memories wide green and yellow stripes (0074) and narrow green and yellow stripes (0075)
- Easy punch rectangle: large (5503) and small (5404)
- Catania yarn: orange (0189)
- Make Me Funny Fibres (9906)
- Pompoms: orange (0509)
- Wooden beads: white (6100)
- Cocktail sticks

Instructions

1. Knit the sweater, transfer it onto cocktail sticks with wooden beads and wind the knitting yarn around a reel made from card. Decorate the sweater with pompoms.

2. Make a double card (10.5 x 15 cm). Cut a rectangle (8 x 12.25 cm) from silvery white card and a rectangle (7.5 x 11.75 cm) from card with wide green and yellow stripes.

3. Punch a large rectangle out of saffron card and a small rectangle out of card with narrow green and yellow stripes.

4. Stick everything on the card.

Pattern

Cast on 8 stitches. Knit 4 rows with Funny Fibres and 10 rows with cotton yarn. Cast on 5 extra stitches on both sides and plain knit 6.5 rows.

Woolly hat

What you need
- Card: cArt-us orange (0545); Cardstock saffron (2090) and silvery white metallic gloss (9201); Making Memories wide green and yellow stripes (0074) and narrow green and yellow stripes (0075)
- Easy punch square: medium (5401) and small (5301)
- Catania yarn: orange (0189)
- Make Me Funny Fibres (9906)
- Pompoms: orange 0509

Instructions
1. Knit the woolly hat and decorate it.

2. Make a double card (13.5 x 13.5 cm). Cut a square (11.5 x 11.5 cm) from silvery white card and a square (11 x 11 cm) from card with wide green and yellow stripes.

3. Punch four medium-sized squares out of saffron card and four small squares out of card with narrow green and yellow stripes.

4. Stick everything on the card and decorate the card with Funny Fibres and pompoms.

Pattern
Cast on 19 stitches. Plain knit 3 rows with Funny Fibres. Knit 15 rows: knit 1 stitch, purl 1 stitch. Thread the yarn through the loops.

Sock

Instructions

1. Knit the sock and thread a cord through it.

2. Make a double card (10.5 x 15 cm). Cut a rectangle (8 x 12.5 cm) from orange card, two rectangles (7.5 x 12 cm and 4.1 x 6.8 cm) from silvery white card and a rectangle (7 x 11.5 cm) from card with narrow green and yellow stripes.

3. Punch a large rectangle out of orange card and a small rectangle out of card with wide green and yellow stripes.

4. Stick the word "Fun" on the smallest rectangle. Stick everything on the card.

Pattern
See page 32.

Yes

Bikini

What you need

- Card: cArt-us spring green (0305); Cardstock silvery white metallic gloss (9201) and saffron (2090); Making Memories wide green and yellow stripes (0074)
- Easy punch rectangle: small (5404)
- Making Memories Funky with Fibres (1705 and 1706)
- Wooden beads: moss green (6702)
- Cocktail sticks

Instructions

1. Knit the bikini and place a couple of stitches on a cocktail stick with a wooden bead.

2. Make a double card (10.5 x 15 cm). Cut a rectangle (7.25 x 11.75 cm) from silvery white card and a rectangle (7 x 11.75 cm) from saffron card.

3. Punch four rectangles out of card with wide green and yellow stripes.

4. Stick everything on the card.

Pattern

See page 32.

Beach bag

What you need
- Card: Cardstock silvery white metallic gloss (9201), grass green (3170) and saffron (2090); Making memories narrow green and yellow stripes (0075) and wide green and yellow stripes (0074)
- Easy punch rectangle: small (5404)
- Catania yarn: light green (0192)
- Making Memories Funky with Fibres (1705)
- Pompoms: white (0516) and yellow (0523)
- Wooden bead: moss green (6702)
- Cocktail stick

Instructions
1. Knit the beach bag. Make a cord and thread it through the bag. Use pompoms to decorate the beach bag.

2. Make a double card (13.5 x 13.5 cm). Cut a square (9.75 x 9.75 cm) from silvery white card and a square (9.5 x 9.5 cm) from saffron card.

3. Punch two rectangles out of both types of card with green and yellow stripes.

4. Stick everything on the card. Use pompoms and a knitting needle to decorate the card.

Pattern
Cast on 18 stitches and plain knit 8 rows. The following 5 rows: plain knit 6 stitches, purl knit 6 stitches and plain knit 6 stitches. Plain knit 6 rows. Knit 1 row with holes and plain knit another 7 rows. Cast off the stitches.

Sweater

What you need
- Card: Cardstock silvery white metallic gloss (9201), grass green (3170) and saffron (2090); Making Memories green stripes (0076)
- Easy punch rectangle: small (5404)
- Frances M. letter stickers: Fun
- Catania light green (0192)
- Making Memories Funky with Fibres (1706)
- Wooden beads: moss green (6702)
- Cocktail sticks

Instructions
1. Knit the sweater, transfer it onto cocktail sticks with green wooden beads and wind the knitting yarn around a reel made from card.

2. Make a double card (10.5 x 15 cm). Cut a rectangle (7.25 x 11.75 cm) from silvery white card and a rectangle (6.75 x 11.25 cm) from saffron card.

3. Punch four rectangles out of card with green stripes.

4. Stick everything on the card. Stick the word "Yes" in the bottom right-hand corner.

Pattern
Use two pieces of yarn. Cast on 8 stitches. Knit 3 rows: knit 1 stitch, purl 1 stitch. Knit 4 rows of stocking stitch. Cast on 5 extra stitches on both sides. Knit another 3.5 rows of stocking stitch.

Bags

Purses

What you need

- Card: cArt-us salmon (0482); Cardstock red (0020) and mango (2130); Making Memories narrow pink and orange stripes (0072)
- Easy punch square: medium (5401) and large (5501)
- Twistart paper yarn: yellow (0212) and salmon (0227)
- Mini bag clips: antique silver (0007)

Instructions

1. Knit two purses and attach the bag clips to them.

2. Make a double card (10.5 x 10.5 cm). Cut a rectangle (7.5 x 12.5 cm) from salmon card and a rectangle (7 x 12 cm) from card with narrow pink and orange stripes.

3. Punch two large squares out of mango card and two small squares out of red card.

4. Stick everything on the card.

Pattern

Cast on 12 stitches. Knit 4 rows: knit 4, purl 4, knit 4. Switch the plain stitch for the purl stitch. Knit a total of 12 rows. Fold it double and glue it in place with the bag clip in between.

Salmon bag

Instructions

1. Knit the bag and attach the bag clip and the handle. Use a rose to decorate the bag.

2. Make a double card (10.5 x 15 cm). Cut a rectangle (6 x 12.5 cm) from card with narrow pink and orange stripes, a rectangle (5.25 x 11.75 cm) from mango card and a rectangle (5 x 11.5 cm) from red card.

3. Stick everything on the card.

Pattern

Cast on 15 stitches and make sure not to cast them on too tight. Plain knit 14 rows. Cast off the stitches. Fold part of it double and glue it down to make a flap. Twist Wire & Wire to make the handle.

What you need

- *Card: cArt-us salmon (0482);*
  Cardstock mango (2130) and red (0020);
  Making Memories narrow pink and orange
  stripes (0072)
- *Twistart paper yarn: salmon (0227)*
- *Mini bag clip: antique silver (0007)*
- *Wire & Wire: silver 26 gauge (2604)*
- *Metal bead: silver-plated rose (9101)*

Red bag

What you need
- *Card: Cardstock red (0020) and lemon (2040); Making Memories pink and orange stripes (0071)*
- *Easy punch rectangle: large (5503)*
- *Frances M. letter stickers: Fun*
- *Twistart paper yarn: pale red (0222)*
- *Mini bag clip: antique silver (0007)*
- *Metal bead: silver-plated rose (9101)*

Instructions
1. Knit the bag and attach the bag clip and the handle. Use a rose to decorate the bag.

2. Make a double card (10.5 x 15 cm). Cut two rectangles (8 x 12.5 cm and 4 x 7 cm) from yellow card and a rectangle (7.5 x 12 cm) from card with pink and orange stripes.

3. Punch a rectangle out of the card with pink and orange stripes and stick the word "Bags" on it.

4. Stick everything on the card.

Pattern
Cast on 7 stitches. Plain knit 28 rows and cast off the stitches. Fold part of it double and glue it down to make a flap. Make a cord.

Girls

Woolly hat

What you need
- Card: Cardstock saffron (2090) and silvery white metallic gloss (9201); Making Memories wide pink and orange stripes (0071) and narrow pink and orange stripes (0072)
- Easy punch rectangle: small (5404)
- Catania yarn: fuchsia (0114) and pale pink (0113)
- Pompoms: pink (0502)

Instructions
1. Knit the woolly hat and stick a pompom on it.

2. Make a double card (10.5 x 15 cm) out of the back of the card with pink and orange stripes. Cut a rectangle (7.5 x 11.5 cm) from silvery white and a rectangle (7 x 11 cm) from saffron card.

3. Punch two small rectangles out of the card with narrow pink and orange stripes.

4. Stick everything on the card.

Pattern
Cast on 19 stitches. Plain knit 3 rows. Knit 15 rows: knit 1 stitch, purl 1 stitch. Thread the yarn through the loops.

Nappy

Instructions

1. Knit the nappy and use a safety pin to keep it closed. Cast on three stitches onto a cocktail stick with white wooden beads and wind the knitting yarn into a bundle.

2. Make a double card (10.5 x 10.5 cm). Cut two rectangles (5 x 7.5 cm) from saffron card and two rectangles (4.5 x 7 cm) from card with narrow pink and orange stripes.

3. Punch two large rectangles out of silvery white card and two small rectangles out of pink card (the back of the card with narrow pink and orange stripes).

4. Stick everything on the card.

Pattern

Cast on 2 stitches. Plain knit 4 rows. Next, add an extra stitch at the start of each new row, until there are 20 stitches. Cast off the stitches. Fold the knitting into a nappy.

What you need

- Card: Cardstock saffron (2090) and silvery white metallic gloss (9201); Making Memories wide pink and orange stripes (0071) and narrow pink and orange stripes (0072)
- Easy punch rectangle: large (5503) and small (5404)
- Catania yarn: white (0105)
- Wooden beads: white (6100)
- Making Memories safety pins: assorted pastel colours (1452)
- Cocktail sticks

Sweater

Instructions

1. Knit the sweater, transfer it onto cocktail sticks with pink wooden beads and wind the knitting yarn around a reel made from card.

2. Make a double card (10.5 x 15 cm) (use the back of the card with the wide pink and orange stripes). Cut a rectangle (7.5 x 13 cm) from saffron card and a rectangle (7 x 12.5 cm) from card with narrow pink and orange stripes.

3. Punch two large rectangles out of card with wide pink and orange stripes and stick the word "Girls" on one of them.

4. Stick everything on the card.

Pattern

Cast on 8 stitches. Plain knit 14 rows. Cast on 5 extra stitches on both sides and plain knit 6.5 rows.

What you need

- *Card: Cardstock saffron (2090); Making Memories wide pink and orange stripes (0071) and narrow pink and orange stripes (0072)*
- *Easy punch rectangle: large (5503)*
- *Frances M. letter stickers: Fun*
- *Catania yarn: pale pink (0013)*
- *Wooden beads: pink (6306)*
- *Cocktail sticks*

Boys

Romper

What you need
- Card: cArt-us cornflower blue (0393); Cardstock silvery white metallic gloss (9201); Making Memories wide blue and green stripes (0068) and narrow blue and green stripes (0068)
- Catania yarn: pale blue (0165)
- Making Memories safety pins: pastel
- Wooden beads: mid-blue (6803)
- Cocktail sticks

Instructions
1. Knit the romper, transfer it onto cocktail sticks with wooden beads and wind the knitting yarn around a reel made from card.

2. Make a double card (13.5 x 13.5 cm). Cut a square (8 x 8 cm) from card with narrow blue and green stripes, a square (7.25 x 7.25 cm) from silvery white card and a square (6.5 x 6.5 cm) from cornflower blue card.

3. Stick everything on the card.

Pattern
Cast on 3 stitches. Knit the rows in plain stitch, adding an extra stitch on both sides four times. Knit 16 rows. Cast off 1 stitch on both sides. Plain knit 4 rows and knit the middle stitches together in the next row. Plain knit 2 rows with 3 stitches on one side. Thread the thread through the loops. Plain knit 2 rows with 3 stitches on the other side.

Blanket

What you need

- Card: cArt-us cornflower blue (0393); Cardstock silvery white metallic gloss (9201); Making Memories wide blue and green stripes (0068) and narrow blue and green stripes (0068)
- Catania yarn: cobalt (0146), pale blue (0165), light green (0192) and yellow (0204)
- Wooden beads: mid-blue (6803)
- Cocktail sticks

Instructions

1. Knit the blanket, transfer it onto cocktail sticks with wooden beads and wind the knitting yarns into bundles.

2. Make a double card (10.5 x 15 cm). Cut a rectangle (9 x 13.5 cm) from silvery white card, a rectangle (7.5 x 12 cm) from cornflower blue card and a rectangle (7 x 11.5 cm) from card with narrow blue and green stripes.

3. Stick everything on the card.

Pattern

Cast on 16 stitches. Knit 6 rows of stocking stitch for each patch.

Sweater

What you need

- Card: cArt-us cornflower blue (0393); Cardstock silvery white metallic gloss (9201) and mint green (3130); Making Memories blue and green stripes (0068)
- Easy punch square: large (5501)
- Frances M. letter stickers: Fun
- Catania yarn: cobalt (0146)
- Make Me Funny Fibres (9905)
- Wooden beads: white (6100)
- Cocktail sticks

Instructions

1. Knit the sweater, transfer it onto cocktail sticks with wooden beads and wind the knitting yarn into a ball.

2. Make a double card (10.5 x 15 cm). Cut a square (7.5 x 7.5 cm) from cornflower blue card and a square (5.75 x 5.75 cm) from silvery white.

3. Punch a square out of mint green card and stick the word "Boys" on it.

4. Stick everything on the card.

Pattern

Cast on 8 stitches with Funny Fibres. Plain knit all the rows. Knit 4 rows with Funny Fibres and 10 rows with cotton yarn. Cast on 5 extra stitches on both sides and plain knit 6.5 rows.

Women

Woolly hat

What you need
- Card: Cardstock silvery white metallic gloss (9201) and violet (5040); Making Memories purple stripes (0079)
- Easy punch rectangle: large (5501)
- Make Me Funny Fibres: 9902
- Wooden beads: dark purple (6601)
- Cocktail sticks

Instructions
1. Knit the woolly hat and make a bobble on top. Make two knitting needles and wind Funny Fibres around them into a bunch.

2. Make a double card (13.5 x 13.5 cm). Cut a square (10 x 10 cm) from card with purple stripes, a square (8.5 x 8.5 cm) from silvery white card and a square (8 x 8 cm) from violet card.

3. Punch two rectangles out of purple card.

4. Stick everything on the card.

Pattern
Cast on 8 stitches. Knit 10 rows of stocking stitch.
Thread the yarn through the loops and pull it tight.

Sweater

Instructions

1. Knit the sweater, transfer it onto cocktail sticks with wooden beads and wind the knitting yarn around a reel made from card.

2. Make a double card (10.5 x 15 cm). Cut a rectangle (8 x 12.5 cm) from silvery white card, a rectangle (7.5 x 12 cm) from violet card and a rectangle (7 x 11.5 cm) from card with purple stripes.

3. Punch a rectangle out of violet card.

4. Stick everything on the card.

Pattern

Cast on 8 stitches. Plain knit 14 rows. Cast on 5 extra stitches on both sides and plain knit 6.5 rows.

Bikini

What you need
- Card: Cardstock silvery white metallic gloss (9201) and violet (5040); Making Memories purple stripes (0079)
- Easy punch rectangle: small (5404)
- Frances M. letter stickers: Fun
- Catania purple (0128)
- Make Me Funny Fibres (9902)

Instructions

1. Knit the bikini.

2. Make a double card (10.5 x 15 cm) (using the back of the Making Memories card). Cut a rectangle (8 x 12.5 cm) from silvery white card, a rectangle (7.5 x 12 cm) from card with purple stripes and two rectangles (3.75 x 6 cm) from silvery white card.

3. Punch two rectangles out of violet card.

4. Stick everything on the card. Stick the word "Woman" on the top violet rectangle.

Pattern
See page 32.

Men

Mittens

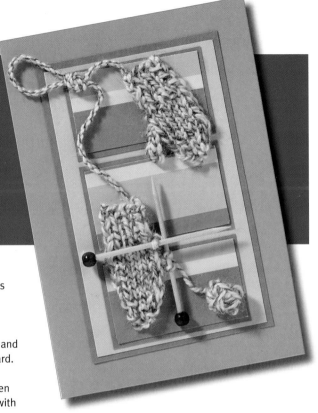

What you need
- Card: Cardstock grey blue (4220) and light grey green (4200); Making Memories blue stripes (0070)
- Easy punch rectangle: large (5503) and small (5404)
- Thin sock yarn
- Wooden beads: dark blue (6804)
- Cocktail sticks

Instructions
1. Knit the mittens, transfer them onto cocktails sticks and wind the knitting yarn into a ball.

2. Make a double card (10.5 x 15 cm). Cut a rectangle (7.5 x 12 cm) out of grey blue card and a rectangle (7 x 11.5 cm) out of grey green card.

3. Punch three large rectangles out of grey green card and three small rectangles out of card with blue stripes.

4. Stick everything on the card.

Pattern
See page 32.

Woolly hat

Instructions

1. Knit the woolly hat and make a bobble on top. Make two knitting needles and wind a piece of sock yarn into a bundle.

2. Make a double card (10.5 x 15 cm). Cut a rectangle (7.5 x 12 cm) from grey green card and a rectangle (7 x 11.5 cm) from card with blue stripes.

3. Punch two large squares out of grey green card and two small squares out of card with blue stripes.

4. Stick everything on the card.

Pattern

Cast on 15 stitches. Knit 17 rows: knit 1 stitch, purl 1 stitch. Thread the yarn through the loops and pull it tight.

What you need

- Card: Cardstock grey blue (4220) and light grey green (4200); Making Memories blue stripes (0070)
- Easy punch square: medium (5401) and large (5501)
- Thin sock yarn
- Wooden beads: dark blue (6804)
- Cocktail sticks

Sock

What you need
- *Card: Cardstock grey blue (4220), dark blue (4310) and light grey green (4200); Making Memories blue stripes (0070)*
- *Frances M. letter stickers: Fun*
- *Thin sock yarn*
- *Wooden beads: dark blue (6804)*
- *Cocktail sticks*

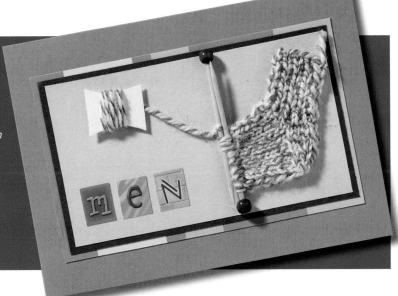

Instructions

1. Knit the sock, transfer it onto cocktail sticks with wooden beads and wind the knitting yarn around a reel made from card.

2. Make a double card (10.5 x 15 cm). Cut a rectangle (7.5 x 12 cm) from card with blue stripes, a rectangle (7 x 12 cm) from dark blue card and a rectangle (6.5 x 11.5 cm) from grey green card.

3. Stick everything on the card. Stick the word "Men" in the bottom left-hand corner of the grey green rectangle.

Pattern
See page 32.

Wire

Bag

What you need
- Card: cArt-us violet (0425) and lilac (0453); Cardstock metallic silver (9113); Making Memories purple and blue stripes (0078) and blue and green stripes (0068)
- Wire & Wire: mid-blue (26 gauge)
- Rocailles: light purple with transparent nucleus (5214)
- Mini bag clip: antique silver (0007)
- Wooden beads: turquoise (6703)
- Cocktail sticks

Instructions
1. Knit the bag and attach the clip to it. Make two knitting needles and wind a piece of Wire & Wire into a bundle.

2. Make a double card (10.5 x 15 cm). Cut a rectangle (8 x 12.5 cm) from card with purple and blue stripes, two rectangles (7.5 x 12.5 cm and 4.5 x 7.5 cm) from silver card, a rectangle (7.25 x 11.75 cm) from lilac card and a rectangle (5 x 8 cm) from card with blue stripes (use the back of the card).

3. Stick everything on the card.

Pattern
Thread Rocailles onto Wire & Wire. Knit plain stitches and slide a Rocaille between each stitch. Cast on 8 stitches. Plain knit 14 rows. Push the knitting together at the top and use jewellery glue to stick it between the bag clip.

Necklace

Instructions

1. Knit the necklace.

2. Make a double card (13.5 x 13.5 cm).
   Cut a square (10.5 x 10.5 cm) from card
   with blue stripes (use the back),
   a square (10 x 10 cm) from card with
   purple and blue stripes, a square
   (6.5 x 6.5 cm) from lilac card and
   a square (6 x 6 cm) from silver card.

3. Stick everything on the card.

Pattern

Thread Rocailles onto Wire & Wire.
Knit plain stitches and slide a
Rocaille between each stitch. Cast
on 2 stitches. Knit one part to be
12 cm and one part to be 15 cm.
Twist the ends. Make an eye on one
end and a hook on the other end.

What you need
- Card: cArt-us lilac (0453); Cardstock metallic
  silver (9113); Making Memories purple and
  blue stripes (0078) and blue stripes (0070)
- Wire & Wire:
  silver 26 gauge (2604)
- Rocailles: bright blue with a silver
  nucleus (5046)

Sweater

Instructions

1. Knit the sweater, transfer it onto cocktail sticks with wooden beads and wind the knitting yarn around a reel made from card.

2. Make a double card (10.5 x 15 cm). Cut a rectangle (8.5 x 13 cm) from card with narrow purple and blue stripes, a rectangle (7.5 x 12 cm) using the back of card with narrow purple and blue stripes and a rectangle (7 x 11.5 cm) from card with blue stripes.

3. Stick everything on the card. Stick the word "Wire" on the card.

Pattern

Thread Rocailles onto Wire & Wire. Knit plain stitches and slide a Rocaille between each stitch. Cast on 8 stitches. Plain knit 14 rows. Cast on 5 extra stitches on both sides. Knit 6.5 rows.

What you need
- Card: cArt-us lilac (0453); Making Memories narrow purple and blue stripes (0078) and blue stripes (0070)
- Frances M. letter stickers: Fun (3760)
- Wire & Wire: purple 26 gauge (2608)
- Rocailles: light purple with transparent nucleus (5214)
- Wooden beads: turquoise (6703)
- Cocktail sticks

Cards on page 1 and page 3

Blanket (page 1)

What you need
- Card: Cardstock saffron (2090); Making Memories wide pink and orange stripes (0071) and narrow pink and orange stripes (0072)
- Catania yarn: white (0105), yellow (0204), pale pink (0113) and fuchsia (0114)
- Wooden beads: pink (6306)
- Cocktail sticks

Instructions
1. Knit the blanket, transfer it onto cocktail sticks with wooden beads, wind the knitting yarn into balls and make a fringe.

2. Make a double card (13.5 x 13.5 cm). Cut a square (10 x 10 cm) from card with narrow pink and orange stripes, a square (9.5 x 9.5 cm) from saffron card and a square (9 x 9 cm) from pink card (use the back of the Making Memories card).

3. Stick everything on the card.

Pattern
Cast on 16 stitches. Plain knit all the rows. Knit 8 rows for each patch.

Chatelaine bag (page 3)

What you need
- Card: cArt-us salmon (0482); Cardstock lemon (2040) and red (0020); Making memories pink and orange stripes (0072)
- Twistart paper yarn (0200)
- Mini bag clip: antique silver (0007)
- Wooden beads: cherry red (6505)
- Cocktail sticks

Instructions
1. Knit the bag and attach the bag clip to it. Make two knitting needles and wind some paper yarn around a reel made from card.

2. Make a double card (10.5 x 15 cm). Cut a rectangle (7.5 x 12 cm) from card with pink and orange stripes, a rectangle (5.5 x 10.5 cm) from lemon card and a rectangle (5,25 x 10.25 cm) from red card.

3. Stick everything on the card.

Pattern
Cast on 9 stitches very loosely. Knit in plain stitch. Wind the yarn around the needle twice for each stitch to create long loops. Allow the loops to slip off. Knit the next row in plain stitch. For the next row, wind the yarn around twice again. Repeat this four times. Fold the bag double and glue it with the seam at the back. Glue a bag clip on both sides.

Patterns

Sock pattern (page 9 and page 27 until *)

Cast on 9 stitches. Knit 12 rows: knit 1 stitch, purl 1 stitch. Knit 10 holes in the next row. Knit the heel using the first 5 stitches and leave the other 4 stitches. Do as follows: knit 4 rows of stocking stitch. In the next row, knit stitches 3 and 4 together. Knit 1 row in purl stitch. In the next row, knit stitches 2 and 3 together. Knit 1 row in purl stitch. Pick the 3 stitches on the edge of this piece. Also pick up the 4 stitches you left earlier (total of 10 stitches now) and knit 8 rows of stocking stitch.*

Next row: knit 2 stitches, slip stitch 3 over stitch 4, knit 2 stitches, knit stitch 7 and stitch 8 together, knit 2 stitches. Knit 1 row in purl stitch. Next row: knit 1 stitch, slip stitch 2 over stitch 3, knit 2 stitches, knit stitch 6 and stitch 7 together, knit 1 stitch. Knit 1 row in purl stitch. Next row: slip stitch 1 over stitch 2, knit 2 stitches, knit stitch 5 and stitch 6 together. Thread the yarn through the loops.

Bikini pattern (pages 10 and 24)

Bikini bottoms: cast on 2 stitches. Plain knit all the rows. Add an extra stitch at the start of each new row, until there are 10 stitches. Knit 1 row using a different yarn. Cast off the stitches. Bikini top: cast on 5 stitches. Plain knit 2 rows. Decrease 1 stitch in the next row. Plain knit 1 row. Continue knitting using the other yarn. Decrease 2 stitches in the next row. Plain knit 1 row. Decrease 2 stitches in the next row. Thread the yarn through the loop. Knit the other half in the same way. Glue the pieces onto a piece of yarn.

Mittens pattern (page 25)

Cast on 7 stitches. Knit 8 rows: knit 1 stitch, purl 1 stitch. Knit 8 rows of stocking stitch. Next row: knit 1 stitch, slip stitch 2 over stitch 3, knit 1 stitch, knit stitch 5 and stitch 6 together. Knit 1 row in purl stitch. Next row: slip stitch 1 over stitch 2, plain knit 1 stitch, knit stitch 4 and stitch 5 together. Thread the yarn through the loops. Thumb: pick up 3 loops on the right side of the mitten. Plain knit 3 rows. Slip stitch 1 over stitch 2. Knit 1 row in purl stitch. Thread the yarn through the loops.

Thanks to Kars & Co BV in Ochten, the Netherlands (+31 (0)44-642864) and Coats GmbH D-79337 Kenzingen Tel.0049 - 7644802222 for providing the materials.